The Mathematical Constant

e

to 100,000 Decimal Places

R. M. Nicholson

Cover and page design by R. M. Nicholson

Published by CreateSpace

First edition published 2017 by CreateSpace

ISBN-13: 978-1548334284

ISBN-10: 1548334286

Contents

2.

71828182845904523536028747135266249775724709369995

95749669676277240766303535475945713821785251664274

27466391932003059921817413596629043572900334295260

59563073813232862794349076323382988075319525101901

15738341879307021540891499348841675092447614606680

82264800168477411853742345442437107539077744992069

55170276183860626133138458300075204493382656029760

67371132007093287091274437470472306969772093101416

92836819025515108657463772111252389784425056953696

77078544996996794686445490598793163688923009879312

77361782154249992295763514822082698951936680331825

28869398496465105820939239829488793320362509443117

30123819706841614039701983767932068328237646480429

53118023287825098194558153017567173613320698112509

96181881593041690351598885193458072738667385894‌22

87922849989208680582574927961048419844436346324496

84875602336248270419786232090021609902353043699418

49146314093431738143640546253152096183690888707016

76839642437814059271456354906130310720851038375051

01157477041718986106873969655212671546889570350354

0212340784981933432106817012100562788023519303 3224

7450158539047304199577770935036604169973297250 8868

7696640355570716226844716256079882651787134195 1246

6520103059212366771943252786753985589448969709 6409

7545918569563802363701621120477427228364896134 2251

6445078182442352948636372141740238893441247963 5743

7026375529444833799801612549227850925778256209 2622

6483262779333865664816277251640191059004916449 9828

9315056604725802778631864155195653244258698294 6959

3080191529872117255634754639644791014590409058 6298

4967912874068705048958586717479854667757573205 6812

8845920541334053922000113786300945560688166740 0169

8420558040336379537645203040243225661352783695 1177

8838638744396625322498506549958862342818997077 3327

6171783928034946501434558897071942586398772754 7109

6295374152111513683506275260232648472870392076 4310

0595841166120545297030236472549296669381151373 2275

3645098889031360205724817658511806303644281231 4965

5070475102544650117272115551948668508003685322 8183

1521960037356252794495158284188294787610852639 8139

55990067376482922443752871846245780361929819713991

47564488262603903381441823262515097482798777996437

30899703888677822713836057729788241256119071766394

65070633045279546618550966661856647097113444740160

70462621568071748187784437143698821855967095910259

68620023537185887485696522000503117343920732113908

03293634479727355955277349071783793421637012050054

51326383544000186323991490705479778056697853358048

96690629511943247309958765523681285904138324116072

26029983305353708761389396391779574540161372236187

89365260538155841587186925538606164779834025435128

43961294603529133259427949043372990857315802909586

31382683291477116396337092400316894586360606458459

25126994655724839186564209752685082307544254599376

91704197778008536273094171016343490769642372229435

23661255725088147792231519747780605696725380171807

76360346245927877846585065605078084421152969752189

08740196609066518035165017925046195013665854366327

12549639908549144200014574760819302212066024330096

41270489439039717719518069908699860663658323227870

93765022601492910115171776359446020232493002804018

67723910288097866605651183260043688508817157238669

84224220102495055188169480322100251542649463981287

36776589276881635983124778865201411741109136011649

95076629077943646005851941998560162647907615321038

72755712699251827568798930276176114616254935649590

37980458381823233686120162437365698467037858533052

75833337939907521660692380533698879565137285593883

49989470741618155012539706464817194670834819721448

88987906765037959036696724949925452790337296361626

58976039498576741397359441023744329709355477982629

61459144293645142861715858733974679189757121195618

73857836447584484235555810500256114923915188930994

63428413936080383091662818811503715284967059741625

62823609216807515017772538740256425347087908913729

17228286115159156837252416307722544063378759310598

26760944203261924285317018781772960235413060672136

04600038966109364709514141718577701418060644363681

54644400533160877831431744408119494229755993140118

88683314832802706553833004693290115744147563139997

22170380461709289457909627166226074071874997535921

27560844147378233032703301682371936480021732857349

35947564334129943024850235732214597843282641421684

87872167336701061509424345698440187331281010794512

72237378861260581656680537143961278887325273738903

92890506865324138062796025930387727697783792868409

32536588073398845721874602100531148335132385004782

71693762180049047955979592905916554705057775143081

75112698985188408718564026035305583737832422924185

62564425502267215598027401261797192804713960068916

38286652770097527670697770364392602243728418408832

51848770472638440379530166905465937461619323840363

89313136432713768884102681121989127522305625675625

47017250863497653672886059667527408686274079128565

76996313789753034660616669804218267724560530660773

89962421834085988207186468262321508028828635974683

96543588566855037731312965879758105012149162076567

69950659715344763470320853215603674828608378656803

07306265763346977429563464371670939719306087696349

53288468336130388294310408002968738691170666661468

Page 6

00015121143442256023874474325250769387077775193299

94213727721125884360871583483562696166198057252661

22067975406210620806498829184543953015299820925030

05498257043390553570168653120526495614857249257386

20691740369521353373253166634546658859728665945113

64413703313936721185695539521084584072443238355860

63106806964924851232632699514603596037297253198368

42336390463213671011619282171115028280160448805880

23820319814930963695967358327420249882456849412738

60566491352526706046234450549227581151709314921879

59271800194096886698683703730220047531433818109270

80300172059355305207007060722339994639905713115870

99635777359027196285061146514837526209565346713290

02599439766311454590268589897911583709341937044115

51219201171648805669459381311838437656206278463104

90346293950029458341164824114969758326011800731699

43739350696629571241027323913874175492307186245454

32220395527352952402459038057445028922468862853365

42213815722131163288112052146489805180092024719391

71055539011394331668151582884368760696110250517100

73927623855533862725535388309606716446623709226468

09671254061869502143176211668140097595281493907222

60111268115310838731761732323526360583817315103459

57365382235349929358228368510078108846343499835184

04451704270189381994243410090575376257767571118090

08816418331920196262341628816652137471732547772778

34887743665188287521566857195063719365653903894493

66421764003121527870222366463635755503565576948886

54950027085392361710550213114741374410613444554419

21013361729962856948991933691847294785807291560885

10396781959429833186480756083679551496636448965592

94818785178403877332624705194505041984774201418394

77312028158868457072905440575106012852580565947030

46836344592652552137008068752009593453607316226118

72817392807462309468536782310609792159936001994623

79934342106878134973469592464697525062469586169091

78573976595199392993995567542714654910456860702099

01260681870498417807917392407194599632306025470790

17745275131868099822847308607665368668555164677029

11336827563107223346726113705490795365834538637196

23585631261838715677411873852772292259474337378569

55384562468010139057278710165129666367644518724656

53730402443684140814488732957847348490003019477888

02046032466084287535184836495919508288832320652212

81041904480472479492913422849519700226013104300624

10717971502793433263407995960531446053230488528972

91765987601666781193793237245385720960758227717848

33616135826128962261181294559274627671377944875867

53657544861407611931125958512655759734573015333642

63076798544338576171533346232527057200530398828949

90342595662329757824887350292591668258944568946559

92658454762694528780516501720674785417887982276806

53665064191097343452887833862172615626958265447820

56729877564263253215942944180399432170000905426507

63095588465895171709147607437136893319469090981904

50129030709956622662030318264936573369841955577696

37876249188528656866076005660256054457113372868402

05574416030837052312242587223488541231794813 88550

07568938112493538631863528708379984569261998179452

33640874295911807474534195514203517261842008455091

70845682368200897739455842679214273477560879644279

20270831215015640634134161716644806981548376449157

39001212170415478725919989438253649505147713793991

47205219529079396137621107238494290616357604596231

25350606853765142311534966568371511660422079639446

66211632551577290709784731562782775987881364919512

57483328793771571459091064841642678309949723674420

17586226940215940792448054125536043131799269673915

75424192966073123937635421392306178767539587114361

04089409966089471418340698362993675362621545247298

46421375289107988438130609555262272083751862983706

67872244301957937937860721072542772890717328548743

74355781966511716618330881129120245204048682200072

34403502544820283425418788465360259150644527165770

00445210977355858976226554849416217149895323834216

00114062950718490427789258552743035221396835679018

07640604213830730877446017084268827226117718084266

43336517800021719034492342642662922614560043373838

68335555343453004264818473989215627086095650629340

40526494324426144566592129122564889356965500915430

6426134252668472594914314239398845432486327461842 8

4665598533231221046625989014171210344608427161661 9

0012571958707932175696985440133976220967494541854 0

7118446433946990162698351607848924514058940946395 2

6780735457970030705116368251948770118976400282764 8

4141605872061841852971891540196882532893091496653 4

5753571427318482016384644832499037886069008072709 3

2767312758196656394114896171683298045513972950668 7

6047409154204284299935410258291135022416907694316 6

8574242522509026939034814856451303069925199590436 3

8402842926741257342244776558417788617173726546208 5

4982944989467873509295816526320722589923687684570 1

7823038096567883112289305809140572610865884845873 1

0165815116753332767488701482916741970151255978257 2

7074064318086014281490241467804723275976842696339 3

5773542930186739439716388611764209004068663398856 8

4168100387238921448317607011668450388721236436704 3

3140911557332801829779887365909166596124020217785 5

8854876176161989370794380056663364884365089144805 5

7103976521469602766258359905198704230017946553678 8

Page 11

56743028597460014378548323706870119007849940493091

89191816493272597740300748796814848823429320230121

28032327460392219687528340516906974194257614673978

11071546418627336909158497318501118396048253351874

84389231772926135430249325628963713619772854566229

24461644497284597867711574125670307871885109336344

48014967524061853656953207417053348678275482781541

55619669110551014727990403868972204655508331707823

94808785990501947563108984124144672821865459971596

63901564194175182093593261631688838013275875260146

05076760983926257264111201352885913178482994756824

72564885533357279772055435681263025357482165854140

00080531482069713726214975557605189048162237679041

49267426000710459226953148351881374638871042735447

67623577933993970632396604969145303273887874557905

93493777232014295480334500069525698093528288778371

06705855677494813738586303857628230406940056653405

84887527005308832459182183494318049834199639981458

77343586311594057044368351528538360944295596436067

60902217418968835481316439974377641583652422346426

19597390455450680695232850751868719449064767791886

72030641863075105351214985105120731384664871754751

83829799901893177515506399810164664145921024068382

94603208535554058147159273220677567669213664081505

90080695254061062853640829327662193193993386162383

60691117677854482361293268581999652392754884274354

14402884536455951247355461394031549520973970511896

24015797683263945063323045219264504965173546677569

92957189896904709027302885449454166997919929480382

54980285946029052763145580316514066229171223429375

80614399348491436210799357673731794896425248881372

04355792875113858569733819760835244232404667780209

48399639946684833774706725483618848273000648319163

82602211055522124673332318446300550448184991699662

20877461402161570210296033185887273332987793525701

82393861244026868339555870607758169954398469568540

67117444493247951957215941964586373612691552645757

47869859642421765928968623835063704339398116713975

44736228625506803682664135541448048997721373174119

19997001729390730335086902092251912444739327837615

63218108428982077069741387070532661176836986477417

87180202729412982310888796831880854367327806879771

65911165422445380662586171172949803824887998650406

15639756299369628093581897614910171453435566595427

57064194408833816841111166200759787244137082333917

88611470822865753107853667469501846214073649391736

62549377830140743026684221503351177364718538723240

40421037907750266020114814935482228916663640782450

16681534121350527857853933260611024980227309363674

02135153864316930152674605360643517321547010914406

50878823636764236831187390937464232609021646365627

55397683401948293279575062439964527257862440037598

34220508089351290231224759706441056783618708771723

33555465482598906861201410107222465904008553798235

25388517162351825651848220312521495070037830041121

62121260527260599443204430562745229161288917668141

60639131235975350390320077529587392412476451850809

16391145929607115634420434713354472098117846145107

78723991406062902282766643092649005922498102910687

59434533858330391178747575977065953570979640012224

Page 14

09219903115822925966791315399156143807012926078019

70225896629233681543124994122594600233994722281710

56603931877226800493833148980338548909468685130789

29206424281917479586619994441119620873049806438500

68526202584328420855823385669366498497208170461353

76163584015342840674118587581546514598270228676671

85530931192334019128617061336487318319756081256946

00894029530944291195902959685639230376899763274622

83900735457144596414108229285922239332836210192822

93724359028300388444570138377163205651835197010011

57220109569978904849644534346121292249647323561263

21951155701565824427661599326463155806672053127596

94853805736420838491888709517605228781733946274764

46568589009362661233111529108160415241002141959373

49786431661556732702792109593543055579732660554677

96355200537830461954063697184291616858273412221714

58858708142740902481854464217748769250933287856706

74677381226752831653559245204578070541352576903253

52273896384749564625594037892492500762438689377647

53101023237467337714745816255306980324990336764554

30305274561512961214585944432150749051491453950981

00138873792637996487372839641689755513227596201183

82486507469854920380976919326064376087432093856028

15642849756549307909733854185583515789409814007691

89238906309054253488389683176290412021294916719581

19357912031625143440965031328352167280213724159473

44095498316138322505486708172221475138425166790445

41661730320082033090289548880851679725849581340713

21805339888281393460498505323404725950972143314925

86604248511405819579711564191458842833000525684776

87430591639049430687134311879618963747550336282093

99493436903210319768981120555953694654247041733238

95394046035325396758354395350516720261647961347790

91232799526492904515114830792336938216601070287265

19381438448445326395173941101311525027504657493430

63766541866128915264446926222884366299462732467958

73638350193714278647139805403821551346322370207153

31348870831741465914924063594930209211220526103123

90682941345696785958518393491382340884274312419099

15287080433280913299307893686712741392289003306999

58759218152976124824091169515877899640903525773459

38248232053055567238095022266790439614231852991989

18106555441247720450851021007152235234279253126693

01082706339423217625700763231391593497099469332410

13908779161651226804414809765618979735043151396066

91325837903374862083669547508328031878670775117752

56639634792592197335779495554986552141933981702686

39987388347010255262052312317215254062571636771270

01076091228152832650898435956897596103837215772683

11707345522501941217015413187936518185020208773269

06133592182000762327269503283827391243828198170871

16810895118789674670707337786959256554271334005232

67060400043488434329027603604980278621607494696549

89210474443927871934536701798673920803845633723311

98385586263800851634559719444199434462476112384461

76157362420159350785208256006041015568898995017325

54337298073561699861101908472096600708320280569917

04259010387692865833655772875868425049269037093426

20280223998618034002113207421986429173836791762328

26444645756330336556777374808644109969141827774253

41701098843585318933917593451157402384729290901546

85591637926961968410006765983997449720472878818312

00233383298030567865480871476464512824264478216644

26661673209601256479451482712567132669706736714461

77956437523917429285039870225837340698523091904649

67260243411270345611114149835783901793499713790913

69670649763712724846661327990825430544929552859493

27938183416078270913266808656559211027337467001325

83428715240835661522165574998431236278287106649401

56467014194371382386345472960697869333597310953712

64994162826564637084905801515382053383265112895049

38566468752921135932220265681856418260827538790002

40791589264602849089492229996616743773134777613415

09652624483327093438984120569261451088578122491396

16912534202918139898683901335795857624435194008943

95518055474655400005176624020282594482883381188638

17495942848920135200909510078649418682560092739776

67585642598378587497776669563350170748579027248701

37026420328396575634801081835618237217708223642318

65915958836694873224117265044872683923284530109916

7751837683159982126323712385435731268120244175401

8521326637405388029012497281808950215531006735818

4430429105288459323064725590442355960551978893259

3033957293466305516043092378567722929353720841669 3

1345752840118737468546916206489911647269094289829 7

1065606801805807843600461866223562874591385185904 4

1625066322224956144872441381384976379710267602084 5

5318241119639279410696194654264800067617276181156 3

0063644321116224837379105623611358836334550102286 1

7051789044057041957785983334846331792190449465292 3

0214692597565663899658937477287513933771055698024 5

5757436190501772466214587592374418657530064998056 6

8837696422982550119506583784312523213530937123524 3

9691496623101103282435700657814876772991609411539 5

4063362752423712935549926713485031578238899567545 2

8791557842048310574933006019795820773955852280730 7

0489509362355507698378819263571417793387502163443 9

1014187576711938914416277109602859415809719913429 3

1329514592437363645647303503737453850348928611314 1

6380947523017450887848856457412750033533034161380 9

Page 19

65600431058605483557739466250332300343415878146346

02169235079216111013148948281895391028916816328709

30971318413981542767881806762865097808571826211700

31400033773015815363341490932370347036375133545376

34521050370995452942055232078817449370937677056009

30635364551091348162737820498565705560878421196403

99723445564586076895155696868993848964391952252323

09703301037277227710870564912966121061494072782442

03341405744144645996823696611887841165629035511783

99440709617725671649197901681952345238074462998776

64824873753313018142763910519234685081979001796519

90705049086523744284165277661142535153866516278131

60909648028012344933724278669308948279134654439319

65254154829494577875758599482099181824522449312077

76825083076828233500159704041919956050970536469647

31424484538258881126027539095488526397086523390529

41829691802357120545328231809270356491743371932080

62873130358964057087377996784517474051531740138487

80828810060463889367116404777559854812639075047472

95012609419990373721246201677030517790352952793168

Page 20

7663050998374418598034988212393409198050551038215

9827677291373138006715339240126954586376422065097

1085290763907972784130176455324752707378876406936

4200121947457023582954813657818098679440202202808

2637957006755393575808086318932075864444206644691

4933446769818081171656866521338968617359245092080

4653125297779661371986959164518694323242464044016

2381978020728394418264502183131483366019384891972

1781715437219210394663847371563022670180134351593

4428538489418256788707212385205972638592249347636

3122188113706307506918260109689069251417142514218

5349153212907772374850663548917089285076023435176

2183550088296474106558148820492395337022705367056

0750317499788187009989251020178015601042277836283

4432372977992993516092588451577205523289697833312

4276712910939931037734259105923032776526676418748

2441076564447767097790392324958416348527735171981

6467383714274297446899232040693250606283446893754

0167878153206160090576934049061461766070943801109

5443261929000745209895959201159412324102274845482
Page 21

05404361871836330268992858623582145643879695210235

26667337243442309157718327756580021192827039104239

19664269111553335945696857828170203254955525288754

64466074620294766116004435551604735044292127916358

74847350159021552212038828116802141386586516846456

99648100156337412550984797301386562754601612792463

59783661480163871602794405482710196290774543628092

61256750718177364174976325443677350363258000404291

99069631173977878750815602273688249670776355598692

84901628768699628053790181848148810833946900016380

79107596074550468891268679281239114888003672072973

08013544313253477130941867171786075229813735391267

72812593958220524289991371690685650421575056729991

27417714927960883150235869781619089490848771772250

38608726183849479397574406649127605188781242336831

25467278331513186758915668300679210215947336858591

20139536030167811041344441103090338876152048829690

91046891676715553733466225455759752026247712427962

25983278405833585897671474205724047439720232895903

72614868838800317414649020384359035852799312387104

2845981608996101945691646983837718267264685264 8691

7294841415300460400429958503516410189902752936 6867

4318349554474581241401907546816077709779205793 8389

5378192128847409929537040546962226547278807248 6855

0804657104312385487335165307057078458424333555 0958

2219128627972054554662670991319023703117796908 9278

6623112661337671178512943059323281605826535623 8481

6419214473254373100206273846681235169101635925 2588

2568064389463898808727352844064622081495138622 7523

9938938734905082625472417781702582044129853760 4998

2789902008349838736299249812574235456843902301 2261

7336658205467856711479730650770354756205674283 0018

7473019197310881157516777005071432012726354601 9124

6080045160810864183553966994693694732227167074 8972

8504641953929664347252547243576591929699490616 7018

9061433616907056148280980363243454128229968275 9802

2669404564218132862451754965214722162083982459 4576

6133427105649571935644315617745008283769357009 9541

9541839029151033187933907614207467028867968594 9854

3978945730076893989007007392469746181285576466 2265
Page 23

41291320405227907121282065377505828004089716346716

37090249067747363091369040026156464321595609108510

92445162454420141442641660181385990017417408244245

37861015843336177729258061115919200841409188819120

88582076270114836717607490469809144430572622111045

83300789331698191603917150622792986282709446275915

00968322634507372545136685817248349847008084016386

82097263713452054398022778663372932908299140106455

89761697455978409211409167684020269370229231743334

49998690184151088899316512509000116371911499485202

48215863962162949817530946230476048323993793910021

42532996476235163569009445086058091202459904612118

62331827861446472779552321863591655188305793065770

33314985100683571356243418818844057800288440181290

31378653794869614630467726914552953690154167025838

03247784227241799451365358226097165258835671213351

95468383353498015032693597981674632318476283063405

88324731228951257944267639877946713121042763380872

69573860931463153914854879251402888502518978807602

38389956156848503919958550292560541767676631453540

58496296796781349420116003325874431438746248313850

21498040168194079568721926846261728740348096793194

99656042991902818105976032632517464050164546062667

65529010639868703668263299050577706266397868453584

38405767329826816344864670743999091750401889231926

75575183540549560177329071272191345775249057715127

73358423314008356080926962298894163047287780054743

79849854556287072996840738293721862383176652471609

09671920072376588942261865504875526145578558987730

08703234726418384831040394818743616224455286163287

62854117594646049702772449079927514644579298254980

22586010017724378401677231668020041625472441794155

47810554178036773553354467030326469619447560812831

93309567968558277193203120594161669390204966535218

96728226719726400294933073847175447537619370178829

76382487233361813499414541694736549254840633793674

36154108159346496043160354435473772880236104774311

53307851599029777714996102746277697596124888794486

09863349422852847651310277926279743981957617505591

30099337736824051090258375934517001534052226614407

72370508900444966132958595360205560340094928209438

62994618834790932894161098856594954213114335608810

23942370608710802646591320356012187593379163966643

72828367523283916888653737513357948598601075693748

89645657187292540448508624449947816273842517229343

96013721240628678363667584533190474395474066401526

08719409157439552827739043038687727282620656631293

87459875317749973799293043294371763801856280061141

61956394241431225439709916356510284831576542703790

68371757648702300523881974987466368562926550582228

87713221781440489538099681072143012394693530931524

05408121570540227441452187654190142838674426001188

90417245705374707555505816328316872471102203537271

66112304857340460879272501694701067831178927095527

25322212522436167334336638475659094972822180941868

40742383515678688934211482039058242243242646436302

01441787982022116248471657468291146315407563770222

74013584110907607846478007018276633622797810454633

11312940448335701348695851652674595151876800333955

22410548181767867772152798270250117195816577603549

73292372473206785369025753623397121688439087887926

21882023055299371323971943330835362312488703864161

94361506529551267334207198502259771408638122015980

89436356180859701008008162255745503910132198197904

55200496185837777210480466355338066165170235950971

33203631578945644487800945620369784973459902004606

88657270186586775784275853064570661712719496737108

39506032675015324359090294915169737381108979347822

97684100117657987098185725131372267749706609250481

87683551600371463868591891301173680521874326542606

37007105953644250627604582523368805525211815664175

53430681181548267844169315284408461087588214317641

64983566312751872818294865565852420685222183075530

61183933269341644594153426517786533979805808281588

06300749952897558204686612590853678738603318442905

51068977869841773560311811167756387258991151680323

65470029879896289861810145964713079161443695646909

09518788574398821730583884980809523077569358851616

02771952148899835863232312730890986156077738600698

40352678267853872159209362558178898134162474864564

33211043194821421299793188104636399541496539441501

38386874838487022468182939186031959866796236348930

92830878407124004310227061375913680565188613134583

07990705003607588327248867879324093380071864152853

31794353507340189119363854673000066045378378447246

92888305469790001312489521004469490320588382949236

13919284305249167833012980192255157050378521810552

96162363752364796268575166006653936414227306300164

86526138918422435017974559936167940633035221118290

71597538821839777552812981538570168702202620274678

64791664403072901844549795639984483680785199708820

14077691992616749911483298218543827189462821653870

64858588646221611410343570342878862979083418871606

21443001453327502971510467315602100004386951058377

37797660034608876248616409386452521779352899475784

96255243925598620521409052346250847830487046492688

31328947055389135729070696759955629858666955972168

65060520728013421043557627791840217976266564845802

61591407173477009039475168017709900129391137881248

53425594931286665346503372884639064996846064474190

75243133239034049081952330443895590605478549546202

63256676813262435925020249516275607080900436460421

49702569148855526502281032776211584228243326952862

91376626754819935461181439133675797001412558701433

19434764035725376914388899683088262844616425575034

00142898255762038636438413790651961291777735418369

46762329829049812617176761915542925704384322399184

82261744350470199171258214687683172646078959690569

98135326443597396517347331948479875806413792688541

35525232757204573294772157068500169500469597583893

73527538622664943456437071610511521617176237598050

90055323215489606281779430226864057955584573060059

83764827033398594200985823514001795071045690191913

59062304102336798080907240196312675268916362136351

03264807723291495085915126581214382337107294914808

84723552863941959934556841563445779517270333742381

29903260198160571971183950662758220321837136059718

02594087061553471310448227271684839552410591360591

98124449784581108545112316681735348382537248253476

36777581712867205865148285317273569069839935110763

43209131978031403165889737962830117840980641017501

65110729329078321774875662893106503838060933728413

99226733384778203302020700517188941706465146238366

72063274264433661217401176691491923557090564480301

63422943018376552631084501725103075409426044096870

66288066265900569082451407632599158164499361455172

45205702044309372230555021722229970620974926860976

27874096264487720560430786348088857091434647932415

36214303199965695610753570417207285334250171325558

81811329550409521783013946521643659426296076857058

56985071571513172629289600725876015648405560886131

65411835958628710665496282599535127193244635791046

55438916515095418730607101503443060958230225745597

49442750676309263225299663382193952029279179732470

94559691016402983683080426309910481567503623509654

92430258957527352141244514954246297225851012070780

21101881067223479725793306531877134384667138075463

83471635428854957610942841898601794658721444495198

80155080404250645219148498992040000731067236994465

52460209087678823000643377256573850109698990581912

90957079866699453765080407917852438222041070599278

88926774575208428752637798673036056123071072392258

15047813791727312612348783340344738335736019732359

46604273704635201327182592410906040097638585857716

95841956310957774852957983684475680312187481820283

39418870763117316152898117564297113341814972180780

40465077657204457082859417475114926179367379999220

18178939943333773114691197073786104196398642216604

55889656832067013375057450388721113324367398402841

88639147633491695114032583475841514170325690161784

93145570690416985805021779849763701475891481054320

58549141006622017217197268789300121012674812702359

40855162601689425111458499658315589660460091525797

88167038462590538325692052042579137894882757960327

88775354668614418268277976512589535637614859944850

49706638406266121957141911063246061774180577212381

65987247243225296909853362844079903000759454628154

92355060864815579289619696170607152015898252997728

03520002610888814176506636216905928021516429198484

07744614361789141519151797653784828268701875003026

48676084332046585254705558824102546548060404373727

71834769014720664234434374255514129178503032471263

41807652518780292553477400110485399696054992650809

39106913376148418348845963656215266103322394174670

64368340504749943339802285610313083038484571294767

38985629393764191440703650754462206118649912724964

37998758065378502037531899726180144046677930501403

01580709266213229273649718653952866567538572115133

60611445722280085118375789921954306341369230229313

97511437024048302273576290399117944992484809150710

02444078482866598579406525539141041497342780203520

13541992597762817818282537202292010818644944834925

54217939827232793570958287485971267807831342861807

50497175747373730296280477376908932558914598141724

85265829951088223005522324221858619139479518422013

15533196343639226842591641686694381225371359607100

31743651959027712571604588486044820674410935215327

90681603205421596795906641112018761853125671015021

22394012856686084694359374081585364819125280049207

24042172170913983123118054043277015835629513656274

6102488277064888650377651756788068724988616570 9484

6665770674577000207144332525555736557083150320 0190

8299209654549873741975660861953349231294026390 4930

9820147003711618294859399311999550704553811967 1128

9367735249958182011774799788636393286405807810 8186

5733766815789382765645064291739668557955505318 8715

3145523530703559947401862259881498546607377876 9878

1542360397080977412361518245964026869979609564 5238

2858423595356461518544816579996460648261396618 720

3048391195602503811115509384202098945915557600 8389

7989949964566262540514195610780090298667014635 2385

3206603257446682025943061880177309110921274113 8269

1487843556793525728088755431646930772353637682 2603

6080174040660997151176880434927489197133087822 9511

2374663263563532851739418946651094374576827078 2209

9284680346841574431277398110441867620329544754 6807

7511126663685479944460934809929518756664999022 616

8601967205374914995122682363789586524546281343 9289

3383651565369924131096381025591146439238052139 0786

2893561660998836479175633176725856523591069520 3268

95990054884753424160586689820067483163174286329119

63339913270908606507459526035715732306971210642342

40815970683287076244371655327502287978025986909811

11226558888151520837482450034463046505984569690276

16695827898291361353530629133142788188824934213644

24178335193197865439402014653280834103417852724898

79050919932369270996567133507711905899945951923990

61515616548030014535921255069640534526382345215599

92105781913710301889792064088397476766714447273142

54467923500524618849237455307575734902707342496298

87999694209459596100870250132945332535804568928570

72412079659198092255050560061971283541270202072583 9

94171175520920820151096509526685113897577150810849

44350828545874991294385756311566832456682799299186

15390092558717168404956639919591540342183645372120

23678608655364745175654879318925644085274489190918

19341166758356343975888604634941311187524103842546

79379992035469104119354431132191360681296575685836

11774564654674861061988591414805799318725367531243

47033548263752708135310557081804964249858464614797

34675993159465147870250652710835087823506565323317

97738656666181652390017664988485456054961300215776

11525581339618402706781490035025287682360782210739

71023391468701597358685890152970103477805032921540

14359595298683404657471756232196640515401477953167

46172620872730482063465246910995332737556109057837

84559454691602236876896414259601646896471063480741

09928546482353083540132332924864037318003195202317

47620653772616371744536054972669060171117676104777

49716668901521638389743117141806222223457185679415

07299526201086205084783127474791909996889937275229

05367478502050003863003652621880067092667410480602

73419977566600294279410904000646542810744540076164

29525362460261476180471744322889953285828397762184

60096766926758127030280651953545205317353680895458

99021807831457758912802039700536331938211000954432

41244197949192916205234421346395653840781209416214

83500115588361842116428399245402759071962153757018

70670837310122461413620489265556681094670763865360

83015847614512581588569610030337081197058344452874

Page 35

666198891534664244887911940711423940115986970795740

59463371702432684848646320189863528270923130470892

15684758207753034387689978702323438584381125011714

01326576932055491186015351955165462794117559396794

79588103339354132897025288935337481062578756203642

94270257512121137330213811951395756419122685155962

47620328203872634206622734786822303652201965572932

59050681348492922996472482293597878427209455782673

29975853818536442370617353517653060396801087899490

50665449154457795216603855239801379810434056418240

33961624949104547121048394392009459146475424247859

91096900046541371091630096785951563947332190934511

83866996462278885581735322132687663495805912376125

12030109838678411957258877992060412600498658950272

47133146763722204388398558347770112599424691208308

59566678753194246513144438997119596810593795753215

55242046594100814183511201741968534326723432718680

99625045432475688702055341969199545300952644398446

38434659883041826293223929561261004588464424428501

15515577659357803795650268061307217586720485417971

57896401554276881090475899564605488362989140226580

02613415803948035797101900415154765501839175577267

78971487934773727475257438981587050407019682151012

18826088040084551332795162841280679678965570163917

06777984152914939740315816789686544884131904636833

21791150591078138982610262719796968264111799186560

38993895418928488851750122504754778999508544083983

80072543146884298841261604268224882309778855649576

54240171145103939279802909976049044288321989767513

20535115230545666467143795931915272680278210241540

62979582882846635562358098672563820056521551995179

35510691277105385526619269035260813677176664350712

13453983711357500975854405939558661737828297120544

69318226040167030853091165797311325951610174919346

82500632857770046869871772552265257084287457330398

59744230639751837209975339055095883623642814493247

46052242405197282515378754196275932743627881928374

02531856685450408939294010405616668676644028682116

07294830305236465560955351079987185041352121321534

71377066768139621144389163240323574157377378790883

82676184587563610264351829518153924552117290229852

78518025598478407179607904114472041476091765804302

98450174686798127758497173173328730528113496959166

83878770723159683343225090702040190305035958919946

66652037530271923764252552910347950343816357721698

11546432924560895115873201267542497571052089436263

95013829621522140336210654228218767395801212864427

88547491928976959315766891987305176388698461503354

59489854184955025169061688841912287338552269997682

26096450075045000961168661291710931802823550425536

53997166054753907348915189650027442328981181709248

27361086380157600724060164954708233134936158243512

82990504054053339925770713210115037138986950767134

47940748097845416328110406350804863393555238405735

58086371876353026186797172560815532871643611147487

51070335129139235954529514074379431449009508099328

72153235195999616750297532475931909938012968640379

78355355907135570836994731192353853105173666915408

73124672334407025250069180267477250789589034488566

73081487299464807786497709361969389290891718228134

00284555251391735597845615035314460340944121151200

17386972614667869337331543410075875149082958227569

19350542184106448264951943804240543255345965248373

78531065797903797750503143647465142248476883132347

97626736898554749442779499165601085282576189643744

64656819789319422077536824661110427671936481836360

53410874897106686631880502655592956812395968044929

51666154098026107816916894187643533634494829001259

29366840591370059526914934421861891742142561071896

84662633587441497697392156639276768772014515330224

18531253084427272457711615055505190762762500165221

66274796257424425420546785767478190959486500575711

01626484783374119804162594081332722990589148642212

79680429847253562372028878300517885397379094552651

35144073130049869453403245984236934627060242579432

56366064059754947123909237245812615458252666730470

23193598665233788562442291882784364404346280948882

88712101968642736370461639297485616780079779959696

84336773035248304747824066992827714006903166070995

14731541919199114531825439062945732986866135248865

00574780251977607442660798300291573030523199052185

71862854368757786091572692523257317166562527427580

84606201770464331012124434092813146597602213604162

23031167750085960128475289259463348312408766740128

17054306798526186894989500491827500830499892647203

49869653633262109198306214950958772282608155667021

55693484634079776879525038204442326697479264829899

01693851155212468893587328987833626781936176402368

17146064951855087805966353546987882050947620163507

57090024201498400967867845405354130050482404996646

97855800262893182651870871461390952145498799230043

17795004895695292801126986325336467371795193630943

99609176354568799002814515169743717518330632232942

19913213761450641139126983712897082939536083288305

02560727275635483742054978566598954690899385589184

41085605111510354367477810778500572718180809661542

70914301016151501308652284223872161810904318316379

60464315231844346697999048653363753192959677260808

53457652274714047941973192220960296582500937408249

71437304008737698806879703804722348882581981902564

Page 40

40868477497675089991641535021602239678163570976378

14023962825054332801828798160046910366602415904504

63733359748811999866399561717108991180985119761648

64992335943282742759833829310998064616053602436040

40848379619072542165869409486682092396143083817303

62152064229783998253369802703993180402492881443064

96147476000876543055716726972591146319906888238930

05380061568007730984416061355843701277573463708822

07379292140954871795694785441495173156182817634392

95702347104600882306375098775213912234195484711969

82303169544468045517922669260631327498272520906329

00327997293290682720464765036696976522767364541903

16398874330422263220213253681760441696120535321743

52764937901877252263626883107879345194133825996368

79502098503302147230760337544234687164722379550779

41303048654034889554002107651716308847597040983313

06109510294140865574071074640401937347718815339902

04703674908435930908635477721056486191860385871588

20244761381603903785326601858425689141091944645661

62667753712365992832481865739251429498555141512136

75828842328595775941268447903691266201530841804173

76989637590025469994541316593419856247807144349772

01991702665380714107259910648709897259362243300706

76047609769045634157657339554958844894809360407715

56887472884518381060690380265283182755603959053815

07241627615047252487759578650784894547389096573312

76385296266451700445962632793463772115102854547231

28800390584059184988338107113660736575369184280846

55898982349219315205257478363855266205400703561310

26040514507932592579822740601219924939173512214533

67079135006074865616573018540492174771620516784865

07913573336334257685988361252720250944019430674728

66798344129301813134429908823400665291538576377911

09557080006001435799563518115967647250756683677260

52352939773016348235753572874236648294604770429166

43840355884642237076011177482107962590118026554886

89951812394706259542545844913402034001964429653706

43088660925268811549596291166168612036195319253262

66227110814214985613264646721195480114245513394638

23859085409178786688269476027818532831554455652659

33912487885639504644196022475186011405239187543742

52658168500305230187709615241165398064678544427312

44621794913065026310629034027372604799401819299544

54297256377507172705659271779285537195547433852182

30949270321834367820638265534115716278860399015749

52080654434094624466346532535815748140224712606189

73060860559065082163068709634119751925774318683671

72213906309306101930318232666642062815512964768531

38610186729218893470393420722455567912395782602489

78371473556820782675452142687314252252601795889759

11623872080758052722103132744475408331921513593452

69613972205646992477182893105883947691708514206315

57192703636345039529604362885088555160008371973526

38383899678918460032707368208323484710847170616087

91952273882523475063808116060908401242224314761035

63328940609282430125462013806032608121942876847907

19254624630905574929878166127191654822964431726358

75245486075630206676569423553427746176355492318174

56159185668061686428714964129290560130053913469569

82949089100399125908829034879194336869694262066294

69485149314726889235716150324055422633916735831027

28579723061998175868700492227418629077079508809336

21534630384296752560436960611019384272388310758777

16535947786814990309787659008695834800431371768329

54871752604714113064847270887246697164585218774442

10090009091618981941345630502895048457582216188739

74439188330855099085660085431027963752474762653530

31558684515120283396640547496946343986288291957510

38478153906834371774071409562833755441356795542466

46013356636173058117116460627178540788984953343291

00315985673932305693426085376230981047171826940937

68675430183701555754082237153803783838334270237953

59344035494521739603270954077121073329365077664656

03712364707109272580867897181182493799540477008369

34888922096381428156159561093181518370113510479017

63835951681446276709034504574609974445001669186756

61035889313483800512736411157304599205955471122443

90319647664276103816428591803748835436066329943689

97300909251776011620437614116166881281782923823112

21745850238080733727204908880095181889576314103157

4476843381004573850085236520693407100789559165498 1

303729294446230637128435798480987196414308514687 85

250331289893195006457225822811754838876710610731 78

169281242483613796475692482076321356427357261609 82

514244526251595251487527380563315096405255265977 69

220778066443381055624435381362589418097880156773 78

951310313157361136026047890761945591820289365770 11

641688170364424269428305745747156749439157359335 37

631148302466687547275666530598197468223465786999 72

291792416156043557665183382167059157867799311835 82

018985573034488368193441830598702188050225919281 80

477752238844071678947804147014146510735804520214 99

197980812095692195622632313741870979731320870864 55

223674041618559079381674565823453530372833095037 290

224298027684515595286569231897980003830613787324 34

546500582722712325031420712488100290697226311129 06

762908095114575806027080609280150440613944635064 30

697427854694774598768210044414534380337597173847 77

232052065301037861326418823586036569054773343070 91

175915258250302941073891444181837877949061313753 67

Page 45

9465489337526032290627763198333797681664172108314 0

55186413330222478711851181703659836596049396457149

16860056567713605331924231852621667602220733688448

44409234470948568027905894191829969467724456269443

30824124384616040828400642486707258366101143340421

44736834536384965447010678273131695384359191204402

83949541956874453676459875488726170687163109591315

80160972238204977257730745456297912790617753166325

28572058587663767542829179335499236782120086019043

69428956102301731743150352204665675088491593025926

61881658100870165849945649558685562820874724831835

15163391892926465588805936012751518382354858934261

65223086697314511412035659916934103076974774451947

04383673960007657862824547206461738080460290363914

44938590124223801733770381546752976455965184926760

39300171943042511794045679862114630138402371099347

24345579473004892982540268082162152234656027425848

65956870745103527942916334059150250759923986112243

40312056999780516223878772230396359709132856830486

16036212757956160132856186638814600472220058001758

0282279272167842720649966956840905752590774886 1054

9380611695429356907737779282108415973746961314 3291

8085104469539734850675905036623917221087323331 6990

9603363771705474725026941732982890400239372879 5493

8654046382859674221631820153013962973439847958 8628

6329347466506902840667190180812655399736759167 9975

9010867483920062877888531102781695087545740384 6075

9461691958461065596332728348560957030557250249 4416

3370665731502371268435819841541031544010084303 8063

1442183776750349813408169325201240813452285974 6267

1517715222306374135925574751353516066910835944 3999

6923158981567320330271292842412196519363037344 0798

1204656795322986357374589031654007016472204989 4456

2905039587378891268056551646427446017473817529 6313

4587393904845604142034264655604221122391346310 2316

1290836446988901247285192778589195228773637440 4326

5926467223998218645279766482667307016880272205 2338

6003728429031558284545938543490994494207509111 0853

2138744823216151007808922516285123275724355101 9990

3819599335003264144605347035729307391257848175 7987

46835342962974965254542686423494927033639942751935

42400019731250988824196000957662572176218604745737

69577649582201796258392376391717855799468922496750

17925191521821962465357557056422822039954668264832

98229961672170801568010807997771265171562742957636

66959661983507435667132218383358509536665806605597

14837677386692255160346364438626997729575065846892

95998091689499818985885295378744895195270977662626

84177088590284321676352132630838812766335363319004

13433284434763006798202371693365365288058015639036

05627227521872724547642588409952164825544536620838

11789117725225682611478014242896970967121967502094

42122627943707332870341064631210055737672745027163

89752341114262878287367583588190567421630615234167

89476056879277154789714326222041069587947186435439

94073863994898683616891937783664832713736365467690

11737602466430822853624947126051732937772472767976

35865806019396287718060679122426813922872134061694

88202950683165458970762366830255616755947749871518

34269892089521826447105149114194411922770109776166

45850068963849426165593473112961064282379048216056

21009426507617383808247903051099879071961185283255

67874729429071510414689481049167510352958972423818

02288151276582257190705537652455285511598636421244

28417625623013953866997030894364590760068493804087

52108541598512780703332077798656359079684621915349

44587677170063778573171211036517486371634098385626

54155557329266461640227979119597524852530037674177

40561257003036258117048383853912072731918450647136

69122576415213769896260940351804147432053600369234

17903544073570305831474162345284018894080898312519

13077418233389818803163391595659545434057777843316

81162551898060409183018907512170192983622897099598

98340548496228428939846984793866861429332454398359

26370366993551842316616152445059805767457653355523

38715678211466689996845227042954589710922163652573

96595028964563776603898803794151791786791067519900

99661392062387323187867584205442793963667591041268

21843375015743069045967947046685602358283919759975

28586538433818912004285378754930276897216819911334

06972822555353000447439588300797997365184591314379

46494086272149669719100359399974735262764126125995

35090260954004866939895589948742137959080289319691

48458268731237101802297753011906842804407809381565

98081694611679374425663244656799606363751546304833

11272223181233837177980043973108740264753658257565

73510599783142648318796198437654958778036852617518

35391844920488198629786329743136948511780579298636

45219323248133939309075456636803851363061971803395

79795225395086974325465026591235850492830288329344

89284591373621624852528877442891851104093746333590

66023323971192281445073558837332405781486266220748

62155133750367755854941386783529282731090038231168

55374520901095101174796663003330352534143230024288

24805139663144663265608158204521688392231202567106

53884595032240023204536338955215399190110352173627

20909565500846486605368975498478995875596103167696

58716128195191966889332664120378475041708175227373

52709893437171676423299569356971662137827361388995

30515711822960896394055380431939398453970864418654

29165585316869753705276070106148802570078538715083

57794809523131527477357117136433564132429742081372

66896149109564214803567792270566625834289773407718

71064986615044747872616424997667148138305394798495

89380642028866679519434827501681920235916332470991

85942520392818083953020434979919361853380201407072

48162730431341898594250385840436599328165194149737

72867295895828819074900403315934360761896096694948

00067194371424058105327517721952474344983414191979

91817990986463158324602151657553175415619894069828

93157458518427833905810294116004986993077514285130

21286202539508732388779357409781288187000829944831

47667818364465651002446782744569559184576806870497

80448241057997107715775790935258038242273776124369

08709875189149049904225568041463131309240101049368

24144925342799220134638053834236964376742886259514

01461782018107341005654667082368543128163390496765

58789901487477972479202502227218169405159042170892

10428755218865830860845270842392865259753614629003

77801670016546716816053432929075730314665624858096

Page 51

3955008002334767618706808652687872278317742021406898070341050620023527363226729196403409357122562365

9496432076928058165514428643204955256838543079254299909353199329432966018220787933122323225928276556

0487633999884784264517318903658797564982076074782702588614099760507880367067322681924735136463567586

1121295307464477714942334386787670582445229660579700713445898759412665460941421144754000721179060745

8330686866231309155780005966522736183536340439991445294960728379007338249976020630448806064574892740

5477306939713370079627461355344425147454236546627522526248699160771111315697253929437567322157587049

5241723242820655322808868670153681482911738542735797154157943689491063759749151524510096986573825654

8995852167472605404683423386107608236057829419480093343700468665682585798273238751583025667201526046

8436141265295651989429118488798681908827733914728206379451226029451570736710563772002342781180262150

2691790400488001808901847311751199425460594416773315777951735444909657521310263068360471403314423

4298077895617051256930051804287472368435536402764 3

9277790863896656639016677662567857535423994742791 9

4425446646433155541382655433884877788599720636796 6

0692327601733858843763144148113561693030468420017 4

3406139522007240365881279824914326173161781389497 0

9550383694795946179798292577409921719227832230063 8

7384996138434398468502234780438733784470928703890 5

3642055747483628461680936365097379090020411852583 5

5252015752392808264625557856581902269583763453426 6

3420946214426672453987171047721482128157607275305 1

7333096345590932366452897801917513298774795292909 9

5980697901485158395404442839883817975112453555484 2

6126784217797728268989735007954505834273726937288 3

8690212528484337091747960320747955408091149186620 8

6871848995504452106161554370832995028549036596173 6

2726552868081324793106686855857401668022408227992 4

3339436093622339032149935726250748061740917363606 2

3654644584763846478695205477195333842034039902447 6

1056010612777546471464177412625548519830144627405 5

3860185570835998154489128686348072071006178705966 9

Page 53

3652186748059435699858596995540893292195072693375

0235821561424994538234781138316591662683103065194 7

3023341938416407682369935766872346221964132251607 6

2611619760347088440464730831726826112777236133819 3

8490606534404043904909864126903479263503943531836 7

4105176256570479706447800468432306943024174902973 1

1819511329357468545504847110787429054998706003739 8

3113761544808189067620753424526993443755719446665 4

5352408828726753775919707452628632284021962955724 7

9329871328524799946389389249432869177701901289142 2

0188747760484939855471168524810559991574441551507 4

3121440612033376286953379243954715539421312102195 4

4305567483704259075530049506649948026147945247390 1

2802842646689229455664958621308118913500279654910 3

4480615017040726801006794892685536094499037392838 3

5206279928201815764270549629974019008374934449506 0

0754365525758905546552402103412862124809003162941 9

7587619594195659255673287423785611266974177136710 4

4248219166714996117289039443936653402942265145756 8

2907490402153401026923964977275904729573320027982 8

16062130523130658731513076913832317193626664465502

29073501734765629303331852094929847522746253456425

67022546957864848199775133263932215794782124933070

51107367474918016345667888810782101151826314878755

13802710137986875129937513330384388563141517590892

89869561975611230253108750571889625357632258342757

63348421016668109884514141469311719314272028007223

44994199900396494824545752070492209162061422291279

53226882390464982390815929611110037569995292512506

73688233852648213896986384052437049402152187547825

16334708243030352103692784976251731782586086221561

45191655734789400195587047847416588473648038659951

19651409542615026615147651220820245816010801218275

98257747765239385915916506744984614916116515382126

67269274612905337531630556544079342787655026673012

14578324885948736899073512166118397877342715872870

91231138347248514603566138218801484056071607465244

11188418007340678985871592739824521473283172146219

07330492060817440914125388918087968538960627860118

19309948924081170235041355412682386374434120926778

17297906947147590182648247611124145564239377322245

38665992861551475342773370683344173073150805440138

89408408725319759553889761398640016563990693460067

07805010585671966367961671400970315351323869728990

01749862948883362389858632127176571330142071330179

99232638198209404299337779034526166589257793139540

51453697304294620794880331410992499071132416945042

41391265397274078984953073730364134893688060340009

64063154070182028924466731505973632131192623117914

27949448972814772640383210217207180175616010251111

79022163703476297572233435788863537030535008357679

18012065301666831678026987386075542374829854824636

09816089576704219031456849429672866463623051017731

32268579232832164818921732941553151386988781837232

27136401175588133252429413534869938465813717585761

43309521476175517083424324341747795792263386634549

59438736807839569911987059388085500837507984051126

65897301814932106195076900758751983686152616408725

25948201269919239167222737184303852631072660000473

67872474915828601694439920041571102706081507270147

6196799714901416392742828895784243980014979856581 3

0305740620028554097382687819891158955487586486645 7

0923172182587034296050820341593880600656184573508 1

8040323477500842141005745773428029854040495555292 1

5986404933246481040773076611691605586804857302606 4

6776425850330183617430641332388770799969864137227 5

5263176496628824679010945311171202438903234102599 3

7511584651917675138077575448307953064925086002835 6

2969704501613793569626675977592343616636937503536 8

6994545503928744499403283281289055605300914164466 0

8691247256021455381248285307613556149618444364923 0

1429093828937321531281879754113921941560663162278 4

8361521406689726610271237157795030621329160019888 0

6369127647416567067485490795342762338253943990022 4

9897288366026392051870479060158408430291478730224 6

6513711443954182534412690033311819142680707351592 8

4180415100555199146564934872796969351992963117195 8

2126262723645800970809916675282036581869911194836 5

8661027583758633229932255414774792104213241668482 6

4953111826527351008031659958888148099457372937856

81411438021523876706455063233067233939551964260397

44382987482232266203635286130254379660094310450015

86048540270367897119346955799891891123022333816023

02236277726084846296189550730850698061500281436425

33666631143332164521388255734632936687095670843225

25643338959978124021641899469783483203760116139138

55499933990786652305860332060641949298931012423081

10580016974597503851688711203774763157731183136000

27425027224515709063044963692309383823291750764696

84003556425503797106891999812319602533733677437970

68771381474755219014292858678172404424804932375033

09570029291266303169705874092144564720227107964847

78657310660832173093768033821742156446602190335203

98153161893578708356160330225516215510717946062189

26743356419600836634838358967034091155130878201387

23494714321400450513941428998350576038799343355677

62802334656585435121936189687683143986673572604086

95111366498812299578016188283412400412614225147 51

84552502502640896823664946401177803776799157180146

38655473326527856941800550136343395350287083622060

51218394185162391537097907680849096741942890611349

79961034672077354959593868862427986411437928435620

575955550014430805126766443218368832143458370854908

22400145857482286068595935026574057509392031358817

22442164955416889785558265198046245527898343289578

41696889075623746728104480301852421770613653323607

38562281666645976540768447159639307820910170907633

77917711485205493367936868430832404126789220929930

41189050175648491749945239377067452457801917184167

95418255543779302992492778924162772577881479747704

46005423669346157135208417428211847353652367573702

35279145983764571225764612260562812785216958089280

89883945944061653405219325148433061053227002311336

80378433377389724881307874325614952744243584753011

15034510373768822383757380428200735858693804433152

92531299610250961137616701875685259212089291313544

73196308440066835155160913925692912175784379179004

80884802302930439263092134276860122655863045691313

35609781567760987118092384406563531361826769237616

13389237802972720736243967239854144480757286813436

Page 59

76800057382396361079622314042949072805855144477133

86823144995479293381312599719968940722338474045425

92316639781608209399269744676323921370773991899853

30148381462236429949390207328507209804090530005916

00916417101756054098143019064443799058312778266257

62288108104414704097708248077905168225857235732665

23441495616900798552084884188602735278086121804941

80600179411471104106887037386743781471612361419504

74056521041002268987858525470689031657094677131822

11320550504657970186933776927825714524883721339461

39878597863200480117928145468590965326166160684031

60077901584946840224344163938313618742275417712170

33615116378235905968516888056130483854208750512693

31441717058805172781279175640532829294273579718233

60842784676292324980318169828654166132873909074116

73461236710905923615511386044724637872124461258040

69317247691522192174090968802090088015356334717756

64392125733993165330324425899852598966724744126503

60841648416072448212598055075485123231333130062149

00427085427359859130413069182792585845094401507192
Page 60

1760479427404774025331430545136771031194754452 1321

7322258755504897992674685415295388714436963994 0639

1099267018219539890685186755868574434469213792 0945

9068367792952824679543730226347249535946630023 5998

9902482998538261403954108124273935302075751287 7427

3992824866921285637240069184859771126480352376 0254

6971430931663653971851462386542167142923619164 7402

1725477872389640431453641905411015143717737977 5246

3632741619269990461595895793940622986041489302 5356

7863350352638206982148700357806110155221022448 6633

2471843670355023266727497877304702161650197119 3744

2505629639916559369593557640005236360445141148 9161

5514777630187630213606882529627446023807752318 9646

8940430331821486556370146924764273954019094035 8443

7251915352134557610698046469739424511797999048 7549

5142201004309023571363689261949376360267364587 2492

9001626755970837979956474873545316865319001764 2722

2751039446099641439322672532108666047912598938 3519

2669449755356809693196264201404278836570261039 0456

1051516117920186989006730270823841032802134874 5672

Page 61

0062839744828713298223957579105420819286308176319

8704828738863906992246184832399290268539249981236 7

0914216134887815012340933879997760974336157509109 9

2585468475923085725368613605356762146929424264323 9

0662670860284616337605157359905086980031423973536 8

9284352949580994344654143161898064514808492926957 4

9412903363373410480943579407321266012450796613789 4

4220848584053644602161651788556896930268518895083 2

4767933004048516889344111258343965904222111527362 7

6278672366665845757559585409486248261694480201791 7

4822308583500786225521635932512576838292497809043 1

1020487089757150333309636515768045019660252155270 8

0352103848176167004443740572131294252820989545456 2

7634435357574167363898010831057993169791791671827 1

1458374352220263877718052502907916454147911736162 5

3155840768495583288190293564201219633684854080865 9

2809513150501260291956257603293251284725046988190 8

1464753243423638638602479439210151923510139011778

9997483527186469346024554247028375300033725403910 0

8599765098764283280290844566202167836226727229273 7

Page 62

7802136524040288172170124909748994544308268617723

9385250883760749742195942655217301733358513894074

5734814416151138084535803974027779507205189348717 0

7229554276836558267067663139119722118115284665022 2

3383490906676554168336907959409404576472940901354 3

5640927796937984206573889148199022539902231591338 8

1458514872251265609275767958737592070139150292165 1

3720851137197522734365458411622066281660256333632 0

7444991851146917445506229714608657873631358538902 3

6625572854245160180804871678236888557532506625426

2367702604215835160174851981885460860036597606743 2

3334641047199102756235864534174863172655639132060 6

4077547794396713836538773776108283000199373597603 7

0467245737880967939894493795829602910746901609451 2

8845655007145809188787954264182014536965996284268 6

8823634958792770070252989609967989759419557352539 1

4237782443302746708282008722602053415292735847582 9

3752248737793789913676464215372784355398624401585 6

4886921016447816616029621135700566383479903340496 2

3875941092886778920270077504951511405782565295015 0

244849682047443797108729431085416845405130163109 02

2671129519591405208275468664181373058379332361 5059

91420452558802135584747515162678153094655412405 240

91663857551298894834797423322854504140527354235 070

33598496459369953495969855424497824958692917918 241

50680530025533704127787034764462443292059068329 018

86692400222391918714603175399666877477960121790 688

62331100290866830543178700935506694438913191333 358

63680374475306645024184371360308522885821217202 312

74167009740351431532131803978033680228154223490 183

73749411797325447859415796210437878707215481409 172

51636154151633813889125885179242377272296034973 055

33840942889918919161186249580560073570527227874 940

32125064542620630446947080427794597381714681039 519

28215506880791367012101099442207370246136871960 314

91162370967939354636396448139025711768057799751 751

29897966707329267488643009739881487378076736379 288

67677811705205343677057315668958991815308257616 065

91843760505051704242093231358724816618683821026 679

97098296643622472364489864897685710017364354733 695

Page 64

56193476385981877568559123762325808493415705708634

50733443976604780386678461711520325115528237161469

20063471357038337722987732136502886886885943405120

57983869370027833123654274505322834626697864469207

80944052138528653384627970748017872477988461146015

07761711626180078155791547230521475994305800665204

27101171256741858602741888013779312799381537276926

12114066810156521441903567333926116697140453812010

04081176012327051316374315448757176876157555491623

66017628802206010686555241416193143126715355871548

66747899398685510873576261006923021359580838145290

64221779298774878416151634949730970079436830508095

56212645927953336906319365944132611179442566024330

64619312002953123619348034504503004315096798588111

89695053733567108633688694466556411266228792181211

41214251673481364724490212752525556476232485056383

91391630760976364990288930588053406631352470996993

36256810236039226404358878755072331988841759052121

13903766092726584090238735534185164264448652478057

63826160023858280693148922231457758783791564902227

59069934648162473439973320601305879606813637815296

46159632606987449611053683842031053641836753735941

76373955988088591188920114871545460924735613515979

99299972229804170711225699631094594509776556640997

27228240152936630948910679632967355058304122586080

50740410916678539569261234499102819759563955711753

01182348030418102908971965527824577028308532173374

15939385958532036455905642297166799003222840812595

69032886928291260139267587858284765599075828016611

12006314541131514410887576708185489428773761899153

76645051642799854510774007719463980462650777766140

53524831090497899859510873112620613018757108643735

74470836621537747097266018865621068151632800090808

61985543035979484798697894664340270292908991434322

23920333487108261968698934611177160561910681226015

87441083309307037750687697748584032413247464376308

78896661519725561803714725900295507184242454051292

46729039791532535999005557334600111693557020225722

44277295026384053830943399938338801883955382154037

14473944651525123546035267423822541483282489901340

23054550811390236768038649723899924257800315803725

55541017846186347869064604586582603607230695257611

31841342252747864648523633247591026705624663508025

53058142201552282050989197818420425028259521880098

84623182851244839305945516200545590777612198129795

40401506539853415790536291017779397769578920845109

79265382905626736402636703151957650493344879513766

26219223718564299915082889808090418918101545081314

50343857340325795497078193852856999262388352215208

14478940626889936085239827537174490903769904145555

26024919012634143132737382707595039088253122353687

63898141825649655632945187096374840743606699125500

26080424160562533591856230955376566866124027875883

10102149528460080480502804525406369128501059991242

12705081331949759171467622673050442250759152902517

42774636494555052325186322411388406191257012917881

38418156691823721540089360347510144855425469893783

42396064608136668297500193791150617094526809847851

52862123171377897417492087541064556959508967969794

98067977096168305794167431051925448632735888511843

65971435833487560274054001655711783091261131173141

69066606067613797690123141099672013123730329707678

98874009931730968738012674053892361223037077972702

51913408503901017399248773524088810408077499244126

35346413181858792480760553268122881584307471326768

28309720314904986888445618797601546823371547841542

97422301665047593933121322565101891753685663381397

36836336126010908419590215582111816677413843969205

87051507425485274481015454107935951359665363004918

87695236775791473191842258068025398184189298889430

38224766186405856591859943091324575886587044653095

33266853226132120982583918053836081414479132031969

92760371947601912866743086152172430498528063801298

34255379486287824758850820609389214668693729881191

56011563370124867540420591146493088821905024885764

57520833639214994419371702685762222510741662309016

65867067714568862793343153513505688216165112807318

52933312407091234383250230234116950174550236050547

58240931756577016048845770177621831846155679784275

41088499501610912720817913532406784267161792013428

90286158327730479483097170553748510938041809149175

02454334322174459241330379283816943309750129185445

96923388733288616144238100112755828623259628572648

12153834890069851150348536954446154216128324170053

35831805200829157229046963655531781523984687254513

06350506984981006205514844020769539324155096762680

88760357246391395527822224643912259265192128844696

11074635861482528200173489575339542550194754426431

48903233373926763409115527189768429887783617346613

53538850765632710781431243501896510923845366023694

02760606421193842276657552106636718796032175271844

04651560427289869560206997012906367847161654793068

86830584650808288661411197913882289811249826143455

94089618135092268576114746094061479372400088421535

35862052780125014270055274468359151840373309373580

49434248394046750570834792794833813327623793784462

92093239994175933749178997864849581488188651491693

02451512835579818112344900827168644548306546633975

25607961593583082140002195161134233705835911154521

72937216640617081316020782133412603568520131613451

3687160098037871255676614392314645808565208403974

2173527448137412152774752022592445615203656082689

0193913957991844109971588312780020898275935898106

8211793615795183793702674145140090283306446620928

5498391692610689751510839631321171285132574349645

0681479694782619701483204392206140109523453209269

1176229813942204430811731739433886796573913576437

6428193536214678374361361615911679265787001377481

7848510041447845416464568496606699139509524527949

1476944103161257577686371363464447700678713106683

4178715562817791223390778412751841931611881558872

9676749605752053192594847679397486414128879475647

3304954355504479027712869009564335791340512737557

3918068223447181679393291214484495538977286966010

7841520390662890781218240141299368590465146519209

9860534778857684269653845944570016975842253124126

0314184562687225811320400564334135243021027392137

8415250475704533878002467378571470021087314693254

5792313475724364054444813209326658298685065912557

7455683288314403227980492741044039217614384057507

0288608423536966715191668510428001748971774811216

841608544544001904492422943336663383476844380726

307319019363571067447363413698467328522605570126

012334836741213572183014684807124185662574285220

091045837273862273007815666689142507334563732595

253354316171586533398433217236881260038090205857

993085557310050877153373744646521187448174886871

523111986911140585034922391567554621424675504986

710264926176510110766876596258810039163948397811

661558519621648769593639890450038325804105442059

828599552390657581080179368070808305189964685408

412752905182813744878769639548306385089756146421

488927129489039802562304681217514550233025408607

158593216034652407639235936999491804707804967644

889980902123735780457040380820770357387588525976

243460885107519933447011274178787884567465664047

016196335467707140905908269542251964094463195476

653032104723804625249971910690110456227579220926

413275369963414576879524224456397301831129145115

227578413203762258624582247846966978594791498161

52262878694413637368312510831068289876612378269750

63430472632784537190244479709750173968312144933572

90791648779915089163278018852504558488782722376705

26381180379247783554001811745295774733971401235201

14599019847533584348612970929285294241398655075225

07808919352104173963493428604871342370429572757862

54936591780540165253633041069203370469109309758878

29382912964478906132000630965607478820821221409784

72301680600835812336957051454650181292694364578357

81560850330339246603955379763083613728949867884285

11398536155933527821037407330768184330408936244605

76706096188294529171362940967592507631348636606011

34611598043414745070551149071664063568873902069027

94534382369305311334409013813928491635074844490768

28386687476663619304123762483801758404678512106 98

29060519611235718881115072360730315850662257456636

67407206689990613206277399411280575979833287879 21

44188725498543014546662945079670707688135022230580

56222594298309688773285678897149462388827218464761

81530458443909672482323482595879636989084566647957

54200195991919240707615823002328977439748112690476

54625687368435222906321788922764328936053594790304

68111141305863482445664891592113822588678809725643

51646404364328416076247766114349880319792230537889

67114805896806159427918964740195498946623296216256

72647390158186929567656014442485018217133005279955

51312539849919933907083138030214072556753022600033

56571593428318265090897935086969895054263584304676

51456689976279896062959251197636729077625678627694

69947280606094290314917493590511523235698715397127

86671807757867191038036899144538148456268260400345

67982486898478111383280549404905197680083202996317

57043011485087384048591850157264392187414592464617

40473527525050678399227312160011716033860471071001

52356311597347111531981987106161098503757589655767

28904060387168114313084172893710817412764581206119

05414595537885320036661526492361003015704462723177

77886498067007235988895287474813721901750747000055

71108178930354895017924552067329003818814068686247

95927220559162790229260059210771051044810339287899

Page 73

1286820705448979977319695574374529708195463924316

6905008398439899303679065554159609932486782475424

3617589443717914037871681661890939002438620386100

1362193667280872414291108080291896093127526202678

8190208559570811185383616612884872952787514320295

3932959105083496870290606928384415225794197648249

6318479414814660898281725690484184326061946254276

9368895354073236342830218969494776612607834632849

3151280615010095391645306145542349233938062140077

9256337619373052025699319099789404390847443596972

5206599901782853767626568355862545269745526099102

5766196140375378595945063632270951224892419318137

8141668427013096050734578659047904243852086508154

9135013649169863904812566661084370229473026672149

1648496107468032615833525803528582757990385840916

7618877199539888680431991650866887781701439663176

1559226201699139661315373802129416000690694753343

6778026322072262658818427572160554614396773362584

2997385077307751473833315101468395296411397329672

5793354039013610739524568624300809672046099554570

974893048753897955544437913037904223460377 6872923

6001386569593952300768091377768847789746299 6994899

4901614186613155220085667369577082272033893 6659590

6663505943300403637625911891956915616261227 0478869

6510356062748423100605472091437069471661080 2773798

4857654348124982244423582832981354364512409 2220896

6439872019979456190303973272546178231363633 7592762

2656301565813545578319730419339269008282952 7182521

3885512658303763047749062599551492594310530 7478901

0430098765808165081448626079751296333266752 5927235

1611791836777128931053144471668835182920514 3436092

9249319118024936605179148533042104389977301 9267686

0853477681495022992809380658400073117678954 9128609

8112311307002535600347898600653805084532572 4315536

5442206766135233740821130783436032694001592 6958459

5882978456494622713008555942933445207270077 1820639

8887404742186697709349647758173683580193168 3221113

6554739228818427137384369052663860766245128 4299368

4350826128813673585362938737923699288370479 0048472

2240370919885912556341130849457067599032002 7516325

13926694249485692320904596897775676762684224768120

03327957705939461318525235645629180590529597479126

61628823814298246226541410672464872161743513173976

97122228010100668178786776119825961537643641828573

48108808998857157027972227473475024843902260788044

80757248077016210646701669651002026543712600466419

35546165838945950143502160890185703558173661823437

49162266907731180012118829973731989100606096684119

32660751654527418294595411892772641925461082463519

31647783837078295218389645376236304858042774417907

16914635654620121512541866488539616154205515237500

04267942534177645908215136752584797744651147504384

60596325820468809667795709044645884673847481638045

63518818321038659479820437633473838901775971423622

30577763955410112945234880983414766455593422094020

59733452337956309441446698222457026367119493286653

98949134422551774640273259672299358133311083171180

72340443268137372312096690524118567348973922341527

50707954137453460386506786693396236535556479102508

52928429422771059305666062515229092414805708097115
Page 76

97834583511731682041296459670706333035692718214962

92272073250126955216172649821895790908865085382490

84890442175553094683205563631643189391762626993103

42894851843925396709224125659330791023654852941621

32200251193795272480340133135247014182195618419055

76103019019952164745973440121160123923567930782319

07702884158146056472914817451053880601097875059255

37152356112290181284710137917215124667428500061818

27127612502524187617748599408452149272790256700592

58544310277046369110988005543124572296838369804708

64041706010966962231877065395275783874454229129966

62301640805476970582141712863632965013041650127815

63977996319574126276340111301350827217722871291640

02237230234809031485343677016544959380750634285293

05313112796594526665196042635040645486254338377220

94284825435368231861829827131824898844982602857056

90699045790998144649193654563259496570044689011049

92393921808815562619183440436226496550644984852161

24984423759284436426120042566286021578011404678796

62339228190804577624109076487087406157070486658398

14484585580327799732792914319578911037353001987311

04868956562819173620367030391797106463099062854837

02836118486672219457621775034511770110458001291255

92546268053742772737886372678301656835109233228064

99084591796203056915668061808265869239205618954216

31986004793961133953226395999749526798801074576466

53837740043746369513368567136255318405463847519164

67379487432709166200980577171034755753331027027063

17395612448413745782734376330101853438497450236265

73319174244656778749966500093870644188673349109987

79260053408624428334504869073382793484253056987374

69497333364267191968992849534561045719338665222471

53668114566659695973507597218841669876732164933189

89671829786579746122165739224048569002253241603678

05329990925438960169901664189038843548375648056012

62883040942132130020616454082198613809946272121432

72344578068199258232028513982371189265412344607235

97174777907172041523181575194793527456442984630888

84638538106862171527453161230316570584897431620983

14013263066998966328885326821452040831107380320527

84669279984003137878996525635126885368435559620598

05727895175449869421932697213320528637457798348731

93888995746342520482133375525845710566195869320315

63299451502519194559691231437579991138301656117185

50881665875675118433814576106036514285842787219023

25981078345939707382251471118783115408757775600206

64124562293239116606733386480367086953749244898068

00021766667482742692596868643373191654871775010634

36083073762816139841073924100371967548338380543698

80310983922140260514297591221159148505938770679068

70135102986220750228772112334562442102471516394125

12589543377884928342363611244738228145045968214522

53550035968325337489186278678359443979041598043992

12488984866079504501170116909251938315560944170539

79006002913150242538482827828262233041513709295021

92196508374714697845805550615914539506437316401173

31780774149755711673303463200840895406654169466574

67357854831337701336289489043976700258630025406352

64006601631712883920305576358989492412827022489373

84890676438533993187860801922310832884745981641770

12640890785517778301316161620497927796705218472127

30327970738223860581986744668610994383049960437407

32319578447325485741623973885201620238478425616351

25971617831068501562991355598747588481510148154909

37380933394074455700842090155903853444962128368313

68737516678051308259459977125746793978149195364287

43211224215798515844916693625515693709168552526447

20786527971466476760328471332985501945689772758983

45058600431682265863117660623720172100792221641018

82993308084093840142137596971859768970427590415009

46595252763487628135867117352364964121058854934496

64589865182654563438285115913763156951989523026288

17949599715452212506674611743948844333126594322867

10965281109501693028351496524082850120190831078678

06706185114574097078756311761074642883559391598542

16731151530969487583789559795861326495698172052842

91038172721213138681565524428109871168862743968021

88558151536753121837411997291947132546519914418850

06720364819759441679508874879344167595983619600109

94838744709079104099785974656112459851972157558134

Page 80

6285461897286150207743745295395369296554490129530 9

7288963767713353842429715394179547179095580120134 2

1017515093149166469905236635023302408721865472762 9

6390657233414550059039138902536993171559171798230 6

5162679744711857951506573868504088229934804445549 8

5059782329789861702949841837625525875745530311299 1

9143411094130882381144430688430626553056016588014 0

8561023324210300218460588586954418502977463085858 4

9613003723819032516222557072997571072730606607291 6

9229780336470488409587112280451885119087185882995 1

4331534128549297173849768523136276076868494780364 9

4829990447571577114108095805814120895605947166862 6

2900361456026253348632849868160394633724366671129 6

4460292915746181117789169695839947080954788863503 2

8112962689923111009988931781531394668188202836836 3

3738222814149740069179421928888171391162839102956 8

4918233358930813360131488748366464224381776081007 7

3918339374934693364474815056493364932315723530610 9

3857968399021533814491269253507682110987383521975 0

7736653475499431740580563099143218212547336281359 4

88317681489194306530426029773885492974570569448783

07794587886506297089549984376018169403105690958714

13868048463598536840341059483417884389631799564688

15791937174656705047441528027712541569401365862097

76073563283296656413581702808801354632610489276873

18299179503799444632815859518138014471681728499967

93061814177131912099236282922612543236071226270324

57263794686353339175873744655200600881997529401757

24212997235420696304278579506089111134165348934311

49175314953530067419744979017235181671568754163484

94949128900173937745143192838243118326326507953037

11778061858511535088099982004827618083072096496364

76943066172549186143700971387567940218696710148540

30747156109135893316560016725212654250289861225930

64841058988471296492309412151445639478899993271458

75969555737090855150648002321476443037232466147111

55257858307102493689881456256878683474551889338518

17916675790542104210363493162578704765431267906612

16644142285017446278477132740595579600648343288827

86483704345606696645689974691037398771289159331327

Page 82

12662475055822586349284277183558316415936677122185

37642376222104779338956378722902509543014182257180

33130014811337773694150848886750189315699484983893

60526668180127839120058014315964419105466632368101

48207799356523056490420711364192200177189107935243

23432276178771256825112648133297435492656868274871

59866549430416484682205939216733594850578496228079

32422649812705271398407720995707236227009245067665

68006914996655573786641187707967754867028786043181

79415217961783106550302871572722822508120170607133

80339641841211253856248920130010782462165136989511

06461113356244383818536627356378343692127935470923

01196559149158005617072585185031672893704119363747

80625824298250726464801821523430268081486978164824

34935345685584369637838415383805118440604369687166

64165140361297299929126308428121491524698774293323

05214999981829046119471676727503742221367186614654

04253446314166064987149900100066004154486843735220

84830594959531828722805208286763003610917345086321

33033647289584176588755345227938480297724485711815

57489356131152492677200636219836998066415954938868

38364118914304437677154980265449590617382655911785

45999378510861446014967645550103653971251138583505

08511244251777292381439623304372403603260318144299

13657502460127875141179449013058034521999927011480

71712847770301254994886841867572975189214295652512

48694398372904741036312189912421733955068877864313

07500248233618327387296973765988200538959029354860

54979802320400472236873557411858132734337978931582

03941287898972897329881255351450764153536051946211

22170006763216111958410292525685365618131387840864

77147099724553013170761712163186600291464501378587

85480209624470377137358772008673805410814004231141

85258032932673963245969140448346657220428806792806

16029884043400536534009706581694636096660911110968

78975180132522447824695791325189212265305608586654

11153735849127902546543690208694198711255884537290

63224423222287139122012248769976837147645598526739

22590499788551425004758526029792930615991344489834

19735833160701075164523013107966203825792785331251

61760789984630103493496981494261055367836366022561

21376708142109137353178068242017573747028718931020

76069533557217043575351774615735248384321015713998

13798596607129664438314791296359275429627129436142

68592213899305498064539914458869247276759854427152

77884438367601499128973582599618697297565889787410

82189422337344547375227693199226359735207229908387

36848434917684119102024662747957956434961501265743

38457586388347358322425353281420478269344731299711

89346354502994681747128179298167439644524956655532

31164992067716366458031820584962613223465260617541

35324447020076618074189140401581485600010301199941

09595492321434406067634769713089513389171050503856

33650354516643177448964006173886176119362267689057

69556939187077039423049400384406226144495725166310

17080642923345170422426679607075404028551182398361

53138375143249305639838187799559494254519675655918

19686908852834348860508285296424375787129294393661

77362830136595872723080969468398938676366226456791

13297746981267522659562100931832208175469477887875

Page 85

5356188335083870248295346078597023609865656376727

5570449525873987181259344190378527557133340984 2450

1272585966924343176890189661454044536790471362 9423

8156127656824247864736176671770647002431119711 0900

0747406594565031537504417798219230632370087203 9212

0854995696810613791890299611789367521460223869 0566

5481382858280449537530160921422195940638787074 7879

9119492089837409178853441752306471503027839797 9864

5173366253295117751055590141604598733381868879 7785

8817291976604516353353556047648420520888811722 8319

9004450428448685233833453010553392963730803973 8230

6047141045254700948994076012152476028199638463 4355

4852932377161410869591950786873276075400085220 0650

3187123927285783580701076254276965535596478945 0166

0138162951779085311398110928315832169315638674 5974

7449584385282701658246192092219529134323496779 3455

8561314020776599614254646328867735689178557683 5169

6083928641888300948832470044795831693153383238 237

7876344426323456301679513671047510469669001217 7771

2806552245368937187145156739473340447280450959 433

Page 86

09068366711065595333860293800099994901064276985962

32604018637335728466795312296831563581454208905406

51226419162015504500430562136991850941034609601030

54381669479596458580442519490511073338767994673447

17186156477238117370356549176287075894560355191956

03962301157866323750234725054461073979402475184415

55817808796282223197269298451668330691950507999335

72591656755572945859621820526504733537123516236627

70479333289322136141858785972771685682725303734836

89191184719713375308844677794327485714882782160884

47657000414034999213767942096275608830815094380307

05666022764678117533361028187800710219794428777313

14638785781720566140902304149992324826898247722210

98521897581408797634861467636063686746119666203473

04608917277240045953051376938375381543486981101990

65170696177405221824742265765213815274061269901270

68808753864086699014617408905409818776718800761241

51967064152117653084325544261017536348281196837493

39582574254124463424723358636077798096019974518775

88454596458959567795588690984047682592534778499304

Page 87

57883128541747079059795909431627722327844578918694

21492945154017421462324030084190797529678244596918

35094742021236179403090486349605340549312999194960

87957952586977170236680033862505764938088740994009

58994810939798323110883876923649022149911112087063

92028924906984353331527279913309863354543249714413

78059132240814960156485679843966464780280409057580

88919025423660677450041341579431211250127523225014

80672329796522304884937511660849761164127773953113

02041566848265531411348993243747890268935173904043

29485161065978583225316820420283499364159598019734

38898830209941521522886111751266861730519562493671

80053845637855129171848417841594797435580617856680

75849108018580569556799018519839766069335822477913

65045627057667351709615504933383904526124043955174

49136885115987454340932040102218982707539212403241

04242445157005296837881574946844150801113861256116

41024771909030500402406622789456070615121082661460

98662040425010583978098192019726759010749924884966

13944118415973461038240117855673908056648332103907

38670832986910780934958288887071106515596512225429

29154212923108071159723275797510859911398076844732

63942641945206313821786226099916008675244626545702

89690671922822830451691113636527745179758421471022

19099906257373383472726498678244401048998507631630

66805026711594463629352512026942481085453060281062

72642365382507733405754757017043670395964677159592

61029438313074897245505729085688496091346323165819

46866058709214465371675565553196209186595262844825

37313536981625173519301153415811713532920358731641

68839107994000677266031617527582917398395852606454

11331898550574784712105350579564909593167216756562

48187820027699637341558800008678525674224615114060

15760115910256449002264980039498403358091309140197

87784365016796016746537028746606258434632970830372

59804946535893189121639760131930794769720580347105

53111117215859219066231028099212084069283091906017

37076465465568341320755631531500645346232100713358

49076330483281534586984973325998011874796642731402

79381289961720524540674695271948079930396730194274

03646659415440009279990863480662233490669522404465

21589928642034350988584226920193405754968409048129

55522654754650713532842543496616084954788090727649

93025270281506786281082524322297998539175984518886

83870044771018667721594397085146646128711487495318

62180941719676843144666435175837688436786081446319

64191256657404771869916091555091087891943125367194

56512618784869108767299105655951551597396590343836

28124629118117760949411880105946336671039049777312

00424357811579042982304507203832278124641367129795

94150829183782132128768905459635863693448797497848

41123274921331663162812456388238288715648447883142

41765014798018785821576879306300115378899801462369

01358037533062461485760749325678076826510457380590

18831237617271889933790487113395588485234240255002

35220061357491431825914247982936777549049639935075

58396689675783643166183693076256035286029406628032

55416535431518013714821941772672244005268401996533

33418400434552529659291850294013160065112439529787

43642228069777204373637178734579484202387451512491

57913139411148608416429347958793681868609689684640

85833413101785814271095541629337591517839234130311

05433287035265999390496682211276815831651124686664

51167351378214345336650598328347443536290312393672

08459316439494188113860797467013470964037853490714

90898423178917397836506547519828833673957143600000

03439863363212091718954899055748693397700245632475

95450441142258241078386683765546740013732432280911

36926706828053975491111661711023974377494793351740

36135005397581475520834285772800986189401984375446

43508149821836011257763244738945205163693858513648

42599645183618569890887217897646947212468079003309

25083496645841656554261294195108847197209106605105

54093373195488840644408028057954900807604003415466

21376696064442937749858973536255919596185524481879

40317374508256072895120945456562159540405425814886

92984278658235767319579928529312086627592236611513

74457679160636216752674404512210510520908347074439

86137829082352772895849625656881972792768694795806

10057378708412144481503479742231210329535929782237

Page 91

71340775495454777918138235426071846171083890978259

64406170543546968567030745411634244134486308676327

94917768292309318322134145548259136720282328439654

90018056532039607955170744960390066969903341992782

12696767771835209083959545341866777944872740383733

38198523588420284015098157959468587453798950325736

28098375922162292585985991238439935755732850286131

55970362934249814178056461615863415338635077223269

99650886087099996489937304930717096788874014974614

75428803874212506892121558766922423874347011209908

59082164073576380817386959755176083877600277517253

03713344565485263566172019756300158004979022341958

67380614424015024362889575032065336908257567855070

20555105572381878574650371086308158185862815883054

56466229769480397061826549138518132673748522718826

79179190913544078526854762541266833982405340224699

89966652573155637645862251862823092085424412805997

62850548891309833176188498335297513607377203057134

27396381265885674050138410747889433939966035918539

34198416322617654857376671943132840050626295140357

87726468064954935574632640818697971863021876002581

39957199236013453742297589182851675113581714726258

28596940798518571870075823122317068134867930884899

27518166139960975310529577358461852586521189333937

57718599163351121634410379104518450190230668930641

78977808158101360449495409665363660370075881004450

26573493512770742674257860878489818562886998085166

57133208358426133811426238554203157742466131088731

06318111989880289722849790551075148403702290580483

05273188495999415660653731402129670222082191586290

59526040406200118152696649100685875926556605675629

63361434230232810747488395040380984981860056164646

09981925761623547871091383296756376150673255086068

34337204387481867916689757465634560200025628896011

91100980453350423842063824039434163502977688802779

83508748117829834941721167491942560160868533243538

59511520618090312416981820793146150620738260971804

58265687043623935757495737332781578904386011378078

50811027304944661182195745017010605938433651945862

83606821085851304998204205784585771759338490155644

47305834515291412561679970569657426139901681932056

24192797728202671429725870019323433787315393940311

54111841014142927417035375420036987606087655001093

45299007034032401334806388514095769557147190364152

02772112707018742154812393195322099750655302264684

42277000205890459227424239049370515073677646298449

71682121994198274794049092601715727439368569721862

93600738707781079744097555662780737122803035004882

98439195464337533557878950640189986850602819024521

91177018634505171087023903398550540704454189088472

04237649974903503851894950589797128663164469940749

09594734115819346183366921695736050815850808379520

36335619947691937965065016808710250735070825260046

82124282043436724582447885925655548786161447871758

10685723568951507076022174335116273317094727659324

13249132702425519391509083601346239612335001086614

62385063312707298774561898438428876409983616496477

57146385732473332665389452358836597295511599051874

11779288608760239306160016168434070611663449248395

15631915288272882283137545867826983069669122013095

Page 94

48159354507549235541677668764552125456812429364274

74153815692219503331560151614492247512488957534835

92622626354540670476703386641002527727680088638326

66294885827403696553293622360905724797947344340777

04284318507901973469071141230364111729224929307731

93930979545287741245118395348038221037364469704696

74930428109117972324486154132640315784309553966710

61468083815548947146733652483679138566431084747848

67624301201848932910961528110808761742277913162934

54944253954227273096450579761228853473931896008109

65202090151104579377602529543130188938184010247010

13492931744356288357860986154569116166985738802497

37569405581386305810998233725651649201554432168616

90537054630176154809626620800633059320775897175589

92586219546209645546462439953539174322822543326717

43084925083964613289295845679273654091199476162251

55964704061297047759818551878441419948614013153859

32206074518590960888428021894335869195960493640965

15703275275706415007762613237836481490052454814131

95989296398441371781402764122087644989688629798910

Page 95

87016427016901400782574831159897633061295119568042

74853178863330411697671750638221352138397791384433

25644288490872919067009802496281560626258636942322

65849062862803505728298310126691910963725837814936

37749605945152169326449451882926395257723484200773

56021656909077097264985642831778694777804964343991

76254921650060862628532947105560267041338450050782

73906402875298641612874964737082351888921896126412

79553536442286955430551308700009878557534223100547

15341281095702487081265431912326195646214937652752

63564021273887651038832550073648999371671832800283

98832319373301564123277185395654932422977953016534

83012849067784503749089174934738901564958857480219

49967226211858743610397749463386330578874874055400

05440439344888192044102134790034598411927024921557

02687370097099520539193097931949588326592217150832

46219423001859743967064911495594117337281998690213

11629886680267446443489233020607003821262841723679

62730719140500808408570397815199814882239005994891

19464744386825337458899623751333782805329282720168

Page 96

1597797006648839448244633221092832050404598300894356595426725687971491870344733823776791482920328319683810590771572719190304236531565095746454964342532806951039655873354980385099514346350617536148005019504520135020018028150693324191826785573776441409708094574562485486770490436836871759091805726979401046501948485314672664297866768769778929143112850504309819294973616594425947175476513520524507259753857795837279770297223143519995849952234404939450211542886724418871740952455477186748491147503180177330468990931797447295703519238768640554427813416980724938221974912425751016218743977290214770463801073147065315420130058381045890500676455733299814994585465510552637491435419586799259598141221873523840795741612337226406386043198893624986764969359256959212849590625444647433175999968516366030521642677042815468177758933925211553859052682331160830275119438482386155285246501032946729719811210531412589816510012074268814357759082522746686320618837683045092178458252623959418967300364080862423365762097911

164176633132885235206248792297895945645033373313 94

223847785827171954123478604343761652415687179435 62

570215636666680088531006728947033079540804583324 19

218848887071227567033317393926250907355616451367 70

641995391119488812406598216857871313850568506230 94

155206877987539740658484250135205615103489821873 77

024506358331424362480743254246419598464741157562 54

410103896715766772631964425249319418064724237893 34

668561083789808830313571333157729435664956078125 30

491759401589514695496522311855966904855946760796 81

901672666346501861829556698939650196145444017681 62

810604465068448139561667220729261210164692339016 79

339963283301316385083096794279293455126843576035 69

019705231383646409613117749046007728408622147475 47

653221505518116489887879087780918009050706040061 22

001005127157599122572528252337802680903052846158 17

395581981223970100920172022516063529224647816155 33

532275453264543087093320924631855976580561717446 84

045004828535339654686267885233004496779558076166 18

018336687923125104608097738955654889628150895196 22

Page 98

09367505884160975228232825043371297018660819374896

86999613014869246944824207236329123670525421454641

62968910442981633373266871675946715392611950649224

72562725454327419349599556959024327909717439225809

81036014863644091014917341830796463450648333034047

65711827040276868271418084574998493392039317445402

61666367464666875438509396712991806747190988531271

07267244285848706943070997565679491984189964257488

84764622030325637751112534060087936904565779272035

20592134592427296520668333851067361527626101602664

77724850833447198919868026561972364208475049626616

07797092906844757798251795569758235084371746103310

38791178923944163011263407753577352055804006698252

31912255705191336314072113497232265491510629617390

50617857127509403623146700931176133132018631158730

88679823929800980508949151078837119409975037547367

43057451872654140164469245767921857536803632891396

64155342066705623272936001177781498886100830877849

57170988085866702310404324252678595556207731054307

22980321259411079573491466846802205018161921507666

4910686203337871382605898765521042366819867017786I

6726719723741569178800016906566590469653161549236O

4061891820982414006103779407166342002735828911994I

82647812782659666207030384795881442790246669264032

79940401680013729347730153094180507058742115328464

22030065507639667561683188970051520266566499294173

82840327305940740147117478464839241225676523593418

55406644098370608363645765708180166428504425822455

16508088644212121139143524539352255221624837917373

30329812349528984098613273709957407786789349311975

20423792502285137588043679185454783641677315182145

72265046408001042021004107660278072915255550321SI

82387221708112766208665317651926458452495269685376

31443799834033694712444724779697389051494112001093

41400737940618594471655166126749307993747057729305

21750426383798367668159183589049652163726492960837

14720406742899627672031541021150433374205718285409

01363257214375920546404718943285486968835997851222

62130812989581571391597464534806099601555877223193

45076031541166311296384371940033373601330552635257

Page 100

14904543279251907940071115047853780363708973401467

53465517470747096935814912797188187854376797751675

92782230031294551859504288390273549467266764750607

26436987613948068790805935317930017110002144177015

04495496412454361656210150919997862972495905809191

82525548635870352932014200585705785541921773050534

26875337990760387466896842834026487332908888817454

53047194740939258407362058242849349024756883352446

21245610156272906513061852073292543417925229941744

78551899950989599998774109514641700769893056201635

02192692653166599093238118295411937545448509428621

83942418621806745712809938525884263193067018209800

80509000198196217584589325168776985941105228454658

35679362969619219080897536813210484518784516230623

91187802460405082490933606999809477625379297359703

77590661459946385783782110171224463558451719416703

44732162722443265914858595797823752976323442911242

31136860372451443876580127159406087878863851108968

08831655050463090061488325454528199082562388058720

42843941834687865142541377686054291079721004271658

Page 101

www.ingramcontent.com/pod-product-compliance
Lightning Source LLC
Chambersburg PA
CBHW062012280526
45787CB00005B/2075